"Encouraging a healt[hy balance of digital] and non-digi-
tal, *Online or Flatline* i[...] [...]at-
ing your website, so[...] and
directories. Choat [...] own
digital marketing to an [...] step
approach using real-world examples."

Mark Ethier
Franchisee and Former Executive of the Walt Disney Company

"Nick Choat has taken the intimidating medium of social media marketing and made it simple. As a small
business owner I have been overwhelmed, and there-
fore not present, by the social media opportunities to
grow my business. Mr. Choat explains this in a language
I can understand. After reading *Online or Flatline*, I am
now excited about implementing this as a part of my
marketing!"

Russell Blumenthal
Multi-unit Team Leader and Owner, Sport Clips Haircuts

"If you are starting a new business or evaluating your current business and are unsure about how to harness the power
of the Internet—read this book!"

William Murray
Chair Emeritus, Manasota SCORE

"Great book, simple and practical. It defines the real
challenges for companies in the digital world."

Rogerio Brecha
CEO, Innovative Management Consulting, Brazil

"The world of big corporations is paved with consultants ready to help in areas and technologies beyond your wildest imagination, but the highway rapidly turns into a dirt road as soon as one enters 'Small Organization Town.' Choat provides us invaluable insights into the concepts, structures, and techniques used by those same consultants and makes them available to entrepreneurs who otherwise would have no resource available to enter and leverage the new digital age."

Alain Godbout
CIO, The Neil Jones Food Co.

"This book and Nick Choat's help with Social Media has been invaluable to our business! My husband and I spent a great deal of time a year ago to find and pick the best website builder and CRM system for our real estate business here in Florida. That was just the first step. Choat spent time explaining to us just what he wrote in this book on how to set up our website material for the best search engine optimization. He also helped by explaining how to use Facebook and Google Ad Words to advertise and attract business. I doubt that we would've been half as successful as we have been this year without his help. After reading this book I have a page full of notes on other ideas and online areas that I need to check out to see what else we can do and improve upon. Thank you for sharing your wealth of wisdom!"

Leslie Gregory
Broker Associate, RE/MAX Fine Properties

"Finally, a common-sense, down-to-earth digital and social marketing guide for the rest of us."

Eric Freeman
Former Executive of the Walt Disney Company

"This book provides a straightforward presentation of techniques and tactics that should be useful to anyone thinking of using digital media as part of their marketing strategy. Nick Choat has an extensive business background relating to technology and data as well as direct experience with using social media to start and grow his new start-up business. He relates the good and bad of his digital marketing efforts in a clear and concise manner that anyone working in the digital space will appreciate. I enjoyed reading this book and learned a lot of interesting things from it."

James M. Curran, Ph.D.
Dean of the College of Business,
University of South Florida Sarasota-Manatee

"Nick Choat takes a subject that for many small business owners is intimidating. His background, context and framework provide the insight necessary for any business owner to move forward increasing market share through digital technologies. As a regular speaker at Station 2, I have seen the direct results of Choat's guidance on our client companies and community members. This is a must read."

Sara Hand
CEO, Spark Growth, Founder, Station 2 Innovation

"Nick Choat's advice regarding marketing and social media for small business has taken my business to the next level. By applying just a few of his ideas and building on them over time I've been able to attract more customers in less time in a cost-effective manner."

John Gregory
Realtor and Former IT Consultant

"With engaging prose and real-world examples, *Online or Flatline* leads busy small owners through the challenges of developing a digital strategy. Drawing on decades of success at Disney and his own small companies, Nick Choat provides a calming, results-focused voice in the swirl of digital social media."

Richard Dean
Media and Entertainment Industry Executive

"The powerful concepts in *Online or Flatline* provide a fundamental marketing framework to drive real results. As a strategic management consultant, I have seen companies of all shapes and sizes try to master the constantly evolving digital marketplace. This book provides practical tools that can transform and elevate any small business. We are all marketers now!"

Shelley Holm
Founder & Managing Director, Forum Solutions

"*Online or Flatline* is a must read for any small business owner. Nick Choat does a wonderful job distilling the complex landscape of digital advertising into simple, actionable steps you can take to grow your business."

Brent Mills
E-commerce Executive

"Social Media and web can be confusing subjects. Nick Choat has done an excellent job in looking at it. His tips are great and using examples makes it very real. A good reader for a novice or for a person who wants to learn more about the subject. Reading *Online or Flatline* could help you move your business ahead."

Andy Fox
President, Fox Business Group LLC

"Nick Choat is an outstanding pragmatic thinker who knows how to take his learnings from some of the world's best consulting firms and companies, and apply them effectively to small business. *Online or Flatline* provides invaluable insights for small business owners and provides very straightforward steps to follow that WILL improve how current and prospective customers view your business. As a business owner, you will appreciate that Nick gets right to the point."

Brian Hartnett
Co-Founder, Strong-Bridge Consulting

"As a small business owner, I KNOW that I have to be on social media but am often overwhelmed by the options and decisions. *Online or Flatline* distills everything down into cost effective and digestible ways to drive customers. I'd recommend this book to any small business that needs more customers."

Martin Wilson
CEO and Chief Marketing Officer, Positive Performance Inc.

Choat, Nick,
Online or flatline :
the small business owner
[2017]
33305239647419
sa   10/18/17

GUIDE TO DIGITAL
MARKETING

ONLINE OR
FLATLINE

NICK CHOAT

Copyright © 2017 by Nick Choat

Editorial Work: AnnaMarie McHargue

Cover Design: Aaron Snethen

Layout Design: Aaron Snethen

All rights reserved. No portion of this book may be repro-
duced, stored in a retrieval system, or transmitted in any
form or by any means © electronic, mechanical, photocopy,
recording, scanning, or other © except for brief quotations in
critical reviews or articles, without the prior written permis-
sion of the publisher.

Published in Boise, Idaho by Elevate,
an imprint of Elevate Publishing.

This book may be purchased in bulk for educational, business, organizational, or promotional use.

For information, please email info@elevatepub.com

Paperback ISBN-13: 9781945449017

eBook ISBN-13: 9781945449024

Library of Congress Control Number: 2016942592

Printed in the United States of America.

DEDICATION

To my Dad and my Grandfather who gave me my first job in their country grocery store in rural East Tennessee. Back then, as a kid, I just thought I was cheap labor. Little did I realize that you were shaping my future for small business ownership.

Thank you.

CONTENTS

INTRODUCTION

I don't intend to bore you with the details of my childhood, but I feel it's important to start the story of this journey and the purpose for this book at a period in my career that shaped my beliefs and poured for me a professional foundation that has spanned many years. It's a bit dramatic to describe this earlier phase of my existence as "making me everything I am today," but it's mostly true.

I also want to declare up front that I'm not a self-professed business or technical guru. I'm just a person who has spent the majority of his career focused on technology solutions that bring real value to businesses. As such, I've developed a lack of fear of digital solutions and a pretty high tolerance for risk and innovation. You may not currently use those phrases to describe yourself, and if not, I'm hopeful this book will help you overcome some of your technical and risk anxiety.

To get us started, I would like to describe what I call the Goodsprings Grocery effect.

Goodsprings Grocery Effect

I challenge you to Google "Goodsprings Grocery." Go ahead and search.

What you'll find is some random noise but no specific reference to a business called Goodsprings Grocery. The reason is that this small business existed long before the advent of the Internet. Computers were more science fiction than real when this business existed. In fact, the concept of a digital strategy didn't even exist.

Goodsprings Grocery (the Store) was a small, country store in rural East Tennessee serving the meager population of the unincorporated community called Goodsprings for several decades. It was the only business in the community. While the Store was the only hub of commerce in this community, this business also served as a social hub where friends met friends, political foes discussed their differences, and sports fans always had a welcome audience. Over those many years of service to the community, this small country store became one of two emotional and social hearts of that community, with the local church being the other.

As proof that I'm not making this story up, here's a picture of the Store the day before the building was demolished:

I know you aren't reading this book to hear stories about commerce in rural East Tennessee. The reason for introducing the Store, however, is that my family owned this establishment for many years. This small community business was my first employer.

My multi-generational family is native to East Tennessee and can best be described as devout, hardworking, music loving, and values oriented. Each generation shared these traits with their children. This ethic to value hard work was responsible for several challenging employment opportunities at Goodsprings Grocery. My siblings and I held fancy jobs like sweeping the floor, pumping gas, sorting deposit soft drink bottles (I know, I'm really dating myself now), and, most importantly, serving our loyal customers.

Along with these challenging work opportunities (hey, things are hard when you're 10 years old), I learned some very genuine skills that have transcended my entire career. The first, most obvious skill was learning how to work and to value work as important. Most of us demonstrate these skills with varying degrees of success. The second skill was an understanding of the economics around small business ownership coupled with a customer service mindset.

There is literally nowhere to hide in a small, rural community, and your market is bound by that same community, so if you want to succeed financially, you have to provide good customer service or everyone in the community will know that you haven't. The final skill was understanding the importance of community and how a small business needs to have a real role in that community. If you focus entirely on the economics and not the community, your business will be seen as inhuman and soulless. No one wants to do business with a zombie.

The Goodsprings Grocery effect has had a profound impact on my career. I owe a much deserved, but too rarely spoken, thanks to my father and the memory of my grandfather for the genuine opportunity to "sweep those floors." I'm truly a better person, and business person, because of that time in my life.

The Misguided Years and (Finally) Getting My Act Together

I can't claim that even after my Goodsprings Grocery years I had a clear line of sight for my career. I suspect, like many folks of my generation and possibly other generations like the millennials, we knew what we didn't want to do but not exactly *what* we wanted to do. For example, I, to this day, respect the opportunity I was given to work in the Store, but I refused to make a career out of the grocery business. It just wasn't me. After a couple of aborted decisions, I did, however, land on an academic career in marketing, which I actually enjoyed. In retrospect, marketing's fundamental premise of understanding and meeting the needs of customers aligned nicely with the skills I developed at Goodsprings Grocery.

Unfortunately, at the time I was graduating with a newly minted marketing degree, employment opportunities for marketing graduates were probably at an all-time low. The job-hunting tipping point for me was when, somewhat out of desperation, I interviewed for a store management position with Kroger. The recruiter was ecstatic because he rarely interviewed a new college grad with about 12 years of experience in the grocery business. He enthusiastically described the fast-track management training program, going into great detail of the department rotation program. What pushed me over the edge was the description of the work in the meat department. I'm not a vegetarian or vegan, but the thought of working in the meat department cemented my desire never, ever to work in the grocery business again.

So, not wanting to work for Kroger or go back to sweeping floors at the Store, I decided to pursue a master's degree. A sane mind would have encouraged me to pursue an MBA, but I guess my sanity during that period was questionable. I'm also pretty unorthodox when it comes to decisions, which probably is both a strength and a weakness. Instead of the MBA, I decided to pursue a graduate degree in computer science, which back then was in a very formative stage.

Remember "punch cards?" I do. I didn't have a Steve Jobs-type of broad vision for how computing would change the entire world, but I did know in my heart that computing would somehow change our lives, as well as the way businesses operate. In retrospect, that degree program, complicated by the fact that I didn't have any background in computer science, was one of the hardest things I've ever tried to accomplish. Along with this hard-earned technical education, however, an even more profound takeaway was that I learned how to learn. Having the ability to stay calm and to be fearless in trying new things—knowing I might make mistakes—has served, and continues to serve, me well.

The career challenge became how to marry my technical and business skills; at the time, the solution was unclear.

Unlike the modern-day college graduate, small business ownership and entrepreneurship were not valid options for entering the workforce when I graduated. The career strategy then was to have your first jobs with large companies, develop your skills in those roles, and then, if you have the inkling, take those big-company skills and start your own company.

So, not to disrupt the status quo around career expectations, I spent the next few years of my career working for large companies.

I began my career as a software developer, but if truth be told, I was only an okay developer. I also found that I wanted roles that would enable me to have closer contact with stakeholders (real people). Fortunately, those early years were formed at the Boeing Company, which offered me multiple leadership opportunities coupled with the training on how to become an effective leader. That's how the big-company roles are supposed to work, right?

That said, you could describe my early career planning focus as opportunistic, so I left the Boeing Company for an opportunity at Ernst & Young Consulting. While I was excited about the opportunity, in retrospect I really didn't know what to expect. Starting with my first client engagement, however, I quickly understood the tremendous learning curve that comes with consulting. Also, you develop client leadership skills necessary to lead clients through dramatic change, many times through their own resistance. Not to oversimplify the value of good consulting, I feel the role of the consultant isn't so much designing the future state for a business as it is helping a business successfully navigate to that future. My specialty within Ernst & Young became how to lead clients through technology development, implementation, and organizational change that either dramatically improved the way those clients interacted with their clients or revolutionized the clients' internal business operations.

This road-warrior consulting career came to an end when my wife and I decided to start a family. To this day, however, I still consider myself a professional consultant and look back on my Ernst & Young days with fondness.

As I mentioned, early in my career I didn't have a clear line of sight for the direction of my career. Along with knowing what I didn't want to do (e.g., write code, work in the grocery business), after Ernst & Young I had developed a much clearer understanding of what I wanted to do. From these experiences to date, I knew that I needed to be close to end consumers to understand their needs and then do what I could to meet them. I also wanted to work on technology solutions that could strategically improve the relationships businesses have with their valued clients. And then I entered the world of "dot-com."

My last few years with Ernst & Young I supported clients in high-tech industries, most of whom were dabbling in some fashion or other with this Internet thing. While very early in its development, the Internet was fascinating to me. I was energized by the potential for those technologies to dramatically change the way a business interacted with end consumers. There was a lot of craziness back then, but I wanted to be a part of that whirlwind.

I spent the next few years with dot-coms focused on online retail and digital entertainment. Those opportunities were somewhat fraught with missteps, but the overall positive direction established how companies do business today. Also, in those roles, I learned very quickly to adapt to change, learn, and grow from my mistakes and keep focused on the future.

Then, after several years in the dot-com world, I received an unexpected call from the Executive Assistant of the then Chief Technology Officer of the Walt Disney Company. The assistant wanted to schedule time for me to meet with her boss to discuss career opportunities at Disney. While I thoroughly enjoyed working with dot-com businesses, Disney presented a unique and truly one-of-a-kind career opportunity. I decided to join the House of Mouse.

Disney, at that time, was facing the emerging challenges around digital media and entertainment, very much like the music industry was several years prior. Unlike many of the companies in the music industry, however, Disney's strategic position was to embrace the migration to digital and treat it as an opportunity, not a threat. I had a leadership role during this transition, which helped me refine my understanding that success with strategic change is probably due to 20 percent technology, with the remainder of the success attributed to working with people and process.

At this point in my career journey, we should pause for a breath. I've touched on several aspects of my professional background that define "me," but let me emphasize some key elements:

- All of my positions (with the exception of Goodsprings Grocery) have had heavy exposure to digital technology.

- I've always worked in roles that had a high degree of risk—risk being defined as the probability of success.

- Most of the projects I have headed have helped change and influence new directions for those companies I've worked for.

- My successes have been because I just don't focus on technology. I instead focus on the business that surrounds that technology. It's the journey to the future state that's at least as important as the future state itself.

After many years in corporate life, I decided to leave that world and Disney to start a new chapter as a small business owner. You're probably thinking that I decided to return to my roots of the grocery business, but I instead decided to travel down the partially paved entrepreneurial route of franchising.

My initial plan was to enter into a franchise system that could leverage my corporate skills and experience. It made a lot of sense for me to utilize those many years in the corporate world where I spent polishing and honing my technology leadership ability. But wouldn't you know it, I chose the hair-cutting industry instead, specifically Sport Clips Haircuts. While on the surface I would agree that cutting hair is pretty far removed from my glory days with companies like Disney. Little did I know how untrue that statement is. Cutting hair is not making movies, but as with Disney, a small business owner needs to obsess over his customers and clients and to embrace, not resist, the transition to digital. And if a small business owner resists the transition, that business could go away.

Let me pause to make this point with a true story to show you how important it is to pay attention to your digital persona as a business owner.

Roughly three months before opening my first Sport Clips store, I was being guided by the franchisor through the opening process: ordering fixtures, getting business licenses, recruiting, and so on. One of the steps was to start the build-out of my social media presence, specifically Facebook.

A related task was to start soliciting page Likes, which is equivalent to building your social audience or fan base. So, I was chugging along slowly but surely building this base, when I noticed on my page that someone had given my store a review, even though the store wasn't ready to open. More odd than the presence of the review was that the actual review rating was a one star with no explanation given for the rating. This is possibly the worst type of review because you're given no context or explanation with which to address the issue. I had essentially been slammed for some reason. This is Facebook, so unfortunately, the whole world could now see this one-star review (including my mom), and I hadn't even cut my first head of hair. Not a great start.

Needless to say, I was in a panic. Should I remove the review and rating? Should I ignore the review? Should I talk to Facebook? As is a good practice of waiting 24 hours after something upsetting happens before you respond, the answer came to me (I didn't invent this answer, however). It dawned on me that in the "real" world, successful business owners don't ignore or shy away from negative customer feedback. Successful business owners engage with those disgruntled customers to understand the issue and hopefully correct the problem.

So, in the spirit of "how would a business owner respond in the real world," I wrote a review response asking if he had any specific feedback in order to help us have a more successful grand opening. As I expected, the reviewer did not reply, but that review, along with my response, is still available for the world to see even today. Take a look at the dialogue in this figure and let me know how you think I handled things:

Like · Comment · about 6 months ago · 55 Reviews ·

Sport Clips Bradenton - Centre Point Commons Fredrik, given we're not open for business, do you have some specific feedback for us? When we do open, we'd like the opportunity to earn your business. thanks

Commented on by Nick Choat [?] · December 29, 2014 at 8:57pm · Edited · Like · 👍 1

The moral of this story is twofold. First, you need to pay attention to your digital presence. You can guarantee your customers, your potential customers, and your competitors—any of those who choose to do so could drop a bomb on you for the world to see. Secondly, while there is technology involved (e.g., Facebook), that technology does not give you the right as a business owner to act differently than if you were dealing with your customers face to face. The error in this is clear. People are watching.

Why This Book?

As you can imagine, transitioning from my corporate roles to the role of a small business owner has had its challenges. I now have to answer my own phone. I have to schedule my own meetings. I don't have free passes to Disney parks. Jokes aside, as a corporate person, I had a lot of both internal and external support for whatever I needed: Good, wicked-smart folks within the company who could produce miracles. External suppliers and consultants who could provide me the perfect match of skills and expertise to solve just about any problem I needed them to solve. Essentially, as a corporate leader, I had an almost limitless supply of human resources to help me at every juncture.

A franchise takes time to open. For a retailer, you have to find a great location, negotiate the lease, manage the build-out, hire good employees, and so on. If I wanted to do a good job, I knew I had to invest some time, especially in my first Sport Clips location. During this time, though, I had the opportunity to do some consulting engagements with a few small businesses in my area. Was that a shock to my system? Coming from the corporate world with abundant support staff to working with small business owners without the same was, needless to say, an awakening. Not to say that these businesses don't employ smart people, but a business with 10 employees can never have the depth and breadth of resources found at companies like the Walt Disney Company. Likewise, none of those smart and hungry vendors who surrounded me at companies like Disney were anywhere to be found in small businesses. Big vendors assume small business means small revenue. Furthermore, I witnessed vendors who supposedly catered to small businesses preying on the small business owners' lack of digital knowledge.

This experience left me with parts of enthusiasm and anger. When working with these small businesses on their digital strategies, I learned two things: (1) all want to learn how to build this part of their business, and (2) simple and direct digital solutions for small businesses can have a huge positive impact. I was really excited about the opportunity to make a big difference. After helping some business owners fend off the digital predators, I became obsessed over what was happening.

From these awful experiences, I developed a mindset, a passion, a mission—call it what you will. Whatever its name, I knew my new mission was to help protect these small business owners and their hard-earned money. I don't consider it a calling per se, but I can help protect small business owners, and I can do that by educating them on how to develop their digital business strategy. They can then defend themselves, and along the way, probably increase their revenue in doing so. I'm convinced education is the foundation for success for both situations.

This book now becomes a means to that educational end. I truly cherish one-to-one discussions with business owners, but in that manner, my reach is limited. While this book will never replace those conversations, it can reach a much bigger audience. Also, the discipline of committing to the written word with the limited page count of a book forces me to surface the highest priority topics and concepts that can have the biggest impact.

A little about my personal style that I hope becomes apparent through my writing:

- I want my voice to be the voice of a business owner who manages his business through digital channels. In other words, I am *you* and not some service provider trying to sell you solutions.

- I am objective and honest. I'm not always right, but I always strive to be truthful.

- I like to have fun, but sometimes comedy is hard to translate into the written word. I can't see if you laugh at my humor.

If you are looking for a digital strategy that defines how to acquire and retain your customers, you have found the right book. While vitally important to your business, I will not discuss more traditional IT needs such as servers, security, or networking. There are plenty of other sources for that type of support. My specialty is around technology that engages and interacts with customers.

The examples I will use in this book are heavily slanted toward consumer-oriented businesses. I own Sport Clips Haircuts, so I use real examples from my experience. Even though this has a consumer slant, these concepts still apply to businesses supporting other businesses. The technology will vary, but the concepts are still applicable.

These are key themes that I intend to weave through this book:

- If you don't have a digital strategy for your business, someone else will create one for you, and you're not going to like the outcomes.

- At least a portion of your target audience is expecting and demanding you to engage with them through digital platforms. As this younger generation ages, digital pressure on your business will only increase.

- The skills you need to define and implement your digital strategy can be learned by anyone. You just need to commit to that learning.

- You, personally as a business owner, need to feel comfortable managing your business through your digital platforms.

Finally, good strategies are based on context. Early on, I'll describe how we get to this point and why digital is growing in importance for business owners. Based on this broader context, I'll then whittle down the thousands of digital options to allow you to focus on what's really important. I'll then wrap things up by teaching you how to implement this overall digital strategy.

Let's get going.

Chapter 1

WHY IS DIGITAL IMPACTING YOUR BUSINESS?

The objective of this section is to provide you a solid grounding in the evolution of digital technology. You'll need a historical context behind the growing influence of technology on business, and you'll also need to gain an understanding as to why consumers now expect to interact with businesses because of this digital upheaval.

I'm going to focus this discussion around digital technologies that have true merit, not just technologies that are cool. The next whiz-bang social media platform might be interesting, but it also might be of no business value. I'll frame this discussion around the generational changes because those patterns ultimately inform our current state.

This high degree of digital change can be stressful, but with some quick instruction and background, any anxiety you might harbor will be reduced significantly. And while you may never be anxiety free, let's get to the point where we reduce your stress enough so that you no longer fear taking the first step.

A Digital Technology History Lesson

Thousands of digital technologies (or more) have been developed over the past few decades. Very few exist today either because they are obsolete or because they never should have existed in the first place. When is the last time you used a floppy disk? What ever happened to Myspace? Does anyone still use a modem? This digital history lesson will describe only those technologies that have had a lasting impact on businesses and our personal life.

Thousands of more technologies will be developed during the upcoming decades. Some of those will be fleeting and disappear; some will make a lasting impact.

While I will discuss how to think strategically about using digital for your business later in the book, you first must learn to respect the past, acknowledge that digital change will continue in the future, but then focus your energies on today. In other words, what can you implement today and why?

I've tried to illustrate with the diagram below those digital technologies that have influenced businesses and consumers. Also take note that the rapid pace of change only continues.

Do you remember mainframe computers, or "big iron"? Mainframe computers are very large, centrally managed computers that I describe as being "hidden behind the curtain." Mainframe computers have been used in industry and government for many decades and continue to be used to this day. The functions they perform of payroll processing or census calculations, while boring, are essential for commerce and government operations. Unless of course you work for one of the very large corporations or government agencies that utilize these computers, we as consumers have almost no exposure to these large machines. Unlike some of the

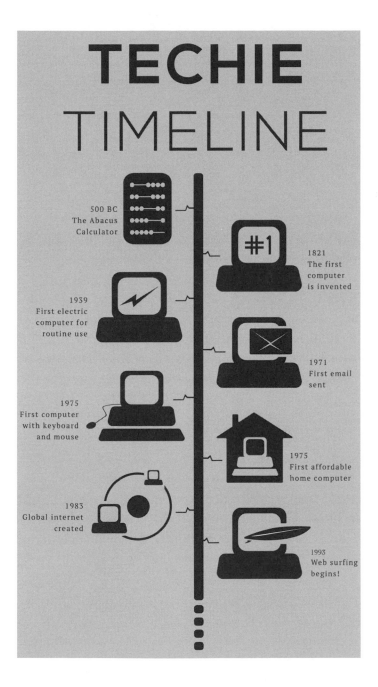

TECHIE
TIMELINE

500 BC
The Abacus
Calculator

1821
The first
computer
is invented

1939
First electric
computer for
routine use

1971
First email
sent

1975
First computer
with keyboard
and mouse

1975
First affordable
home computer

1983
Global internet
created

1993
Web surfing
begins!

more modern technologies, mainframes didn't influence consumer behavior. Mainframes did, however, pave the way for those more modern technologies to exist.

The next generation of digital change was the introduction of personal computing (PC), which I consider digital "for the people." For the first time, consumers and small businesses had access to digital solutions. Personal computing brought digital technology out from behind the curtain and dropped it smack dab on your desk. The first PCs were pretty humble devices by today's standards. Back then, you could do things such as play games, maybe create a spreadsheet to balance your checkbook, or have a digital way to store your recipes. Eventually, software developers started to create new applications that increased the value of that expensive piece of hardware you only used to play Pong. Along with being a technology "for the people," the pace of change was fueled by software, not hardware, for the first time. That's why modern-day PCs and laptops still exist.

The next seismic digital shift was the digital generation that connected all of us. The Internet, which is the technology that powers the World Wide Web, was created several decades ago, mostly for military and academic research purposes. The Internet came out of the labs with the introduction of personal computing, and the World Wide Web was born. The World Wide Web enabled e-commerce companies to exist. Do you remember when Amazon.com only sold books? Do you remember when Pets.com thought it was a great idea to let you buy dog food over the Web and have it shipped to your home? Do you remember when this company named Google didn't exist? The World Wide Web generated a lot of innovation — along with some general craziness. The end result, however, was that all businesses and consumers had the ability to connect to a larger body of technology.

Next came the always-connected generation. The original cell phones were just a portable and untethered way to make phone calls. This was truly cool, but when some smart people combined phone calls with the connectivity of the World Wide Web, they created smartphones and tablet devices. You now have digitally fueled individuals who have computing power at their fingertips and available to them anywhere. As consumers today, we are carrying more digital horsepower in our pockets than most businesses had available even 20 or 30 years ago.

Our final strategic stop on this digital history lesson is social media. Social media is a very broad classification of digital capability where consumers, and now businesses, can interact with each other socially. Notable company names like Facebook and Twitter dominate this space. Many business owners have expressed to me that they don't get the point of social media for business purposes. But before you completely dismiss social media, let me explain how social media platforms have become so dominant.

First, people enjoy using social media platforms like Facebook. Likewise, social media platforms aren't hidden behind the curtain and are available to all businesses and consumers. Finally, these social media platforms are optimized for mobile devices, such as smartphones and tablets, which enable us to be "social on the go."

Social media platforms are truly strategic. Why then is it that social media is so misunderstood, especially by business owners? Business owners are generally not stupid people. Why then have the "light bulbs" not been turned on? The answer oftentimes is driven by generational differences and caused by a lack of good examples that illustrate true business value.

The Dawn of the Digital Generation

Starting back in the 1960s, several researchers studied how new technologies, or innovations in general, have been adopted by society. While these adoption models are perfectly fine, they are a touch academic and not very practical for day-to-day decision-making. So, at the risk of oversimplifying digital adoption, I would like to suggest a more direct and practical model.

As I discussed in the prior chapter, our society has experienced multiple insertions of strategic technologies into our business and personal lives. When I think about those technologies and their inception, I can identify several patterns.

First and foremost, digital adoption is not related to personal capabilities. We're all relatively smart people. Digital adoption, instead, is driven by two factors that all of us can control and influence.

The first factor is a generational exposure factor that results in *comfort*. Every generation has been exposed to a set of technologies. If, for example, someone was born in the 21st century, he's been heavily exposed to

the World Wide Web and mobile device. So, under-
standably, that generation is very comfortable using that
technology.

Someone born in the 1940s has been exposed to those
same technologies but only recently. That person born
in the 1940s will not be as comfortable because he or
she didn't grow up being surrounded by those technologies. Are those born in the 1940s capable of learning
that technology? Absolutely, assuming they believe they
can overcome the natural discomfort.

Value understanding is the second factor driving
comfort. Just being exposed to a digital solution isn't
sufficient. For example, I've been exposed to Twitter, but
I have yet to understand how it could support either my
personal or business needs. A person who truly adopts
a digital solution has a pretty accurate understanding
of why one should use that technology. I consider this
factor the motivation to use a technology. I don't intend
to launch you down this trail of trying all technologies
until you find something that works, however. Instead,
I intend to jump-start your value understanding by giv-
ing you specific recommendations to guide you on this
journey.

To summarize: digital adoption = comfort (belief) +
value understanding (motivation). If, for example, you
want to use Facebook for your business, you first need
to believe you can learn the tool, and second, you need
to be motivated to learn because of the expected value
you will receive.

Here's one of my life lessons to make this point. I'm
not going to give my age, but you could safely assume

that I haven't been surrounded by social media my whole life.

Before I became a Sport Clips owner, I was the worst with Facebook. I would make maybe one or two posts per year, so my personal Facebook page was, and still is, pretty bland and boring.

After becoming a Sport Clips owner, I quickly realized that haircuts are very personal. For 20 minutes once a month or so, our customers let another person touch their hair. After that haircut, the person reenters the world with a new haircut that all acquaintances will be exposed to for the next 30 days. I'm rarely in the store, so I can't physically talk to each and every customer to hear the feedback. I have learned, however, that I can communicate to the customers through Facebook and have experimented with many approaches. I posted the "corporate" type of content with limited results. However, when I spoke to my Facebook audience as a human, folks responded. Humans care for other humans, which a business can't. So just show your human side, and you'll be surprised by what happens. Believe me, this stuff isn't complicated.

I went from a person who was awful with Facebook to a person who is now better than awful. Was this transition frustrating? Making mistakes is never fun. Was I fearful during this transition? You better believe I was. Knowing what I know now, would I have done things differently? The answer to that question is absolutely not. Even with my technology background, frustration and anxiety are unfortunately necessary to learn and master these solutions. To be successful, you need to be patient and accept that this is normal.

Regardless of your generation, you too can learn and prosper with these newer digital solutions.

What's All the Fuss over the Millennial Generation?

There's a lot of chatter around the millennial generation. There also seems to be a lot of angst around how to service their needs as consumers. Oddly enough, I've been around long enough to recognize there's always angst when an older generation tries to understand a newer generation. It's time to get over the angst and accept the fact that you just need to understand how to service their needs. It's no different than trying to understand the needs of the 65-plus age group.

Here's the digital truth about millennials. They've been exposed to technologies their whole life, which means that things like mobile devices and social media come very naturally to them. Because of this comfort, they expect to have their needs satisfied with that same set of technologies. If you as a business owner choose not to use those technologies, you run the serious risk of not having millennials as your customers.

The millennials are just a more extreme example of a target market with strong digital needs. I'm convinced, though, that the digital needs of all target markets are increasing. If you remember our history lesson, this transition is very consistent with early generations of technologies.

Remember the secret formula and all will be well: digital adoption = comfort (belief) + value understanding (motivation).

Chapter 2
WHAT'S OLD IS NEW AND WHAT'S NEW IS OLD

Throughout the course of my career, and even today, I continue to encounter folks who are apprehensive about technology. You hear comments such as, "I'm not a techie," which I trust is true to some degree. It's human nature to be apprehensive of new things. I feel strongly, however, that this apprehension is self-induced and that everyone can learn.

When presented with the next new technical "thing," you have two choices: either fly away from the solution or fight the apprehension gene and try something new. With the first option, you'll remain in your current state, and if you're a business owner, your business will not advance, grow, or remain relevant. With the second option, your business will be able to harvest these new benefits.

Human nature is hard to overcome. It's especially hard to overcome if you don't have guidance on how to move into this new future. This chapter is intended to be that first nudge that you can use to resist and fight off your inherent apprehension. All I need from you is an open mind and a willingness to learn.

Universal Truth: Technology Is Based on Evolution, Not Invention

I'm going out on a limb to make a point. There has never been, in the history of computing technologies, anything that was ever invented. Invention is that aha moment when something didn't exist yesterday but does now. Has there been innovation? Absolutely! Have we ever witnessed innovation that fundamentally changed our lives and our businesses? You better believe it! Innovation, however, isn't invention. Innovation is a constant and continual state of evolution. Trying things and learning from successes and failures.

This illustration is so true:

As an example, Facebook did not create the social concept. Humans have been social from the beginning of time. Facebook has just provided another venue for being social, but it will never replace face-to-face social activity. What Facebook has accomplished is a means to amplify our ability to be social, or give us "social at scale." Now when we speak in Facebook, all of our friends can listen and participate. Whether you like or even use Facebook isn't the point. What Facebook has built is a new mechanism for anyone to reach a large social audience with very little extra effort. Facebook is a great example of innovation built on a timeless concept called "social."

As another example, consider the iPhone. The iPhone was introduced to the world at a specific time. But there wasn't any one person or team of people who woke up one morning and decided they wanted to build this wonderful device.

The iPhone started with an Apple product introduced in the 1990s called the Newton. The Newton was
Apple's version of a Personal Digital Assistant (PDA).
A PDA was a digital device to manage things such as
your task list, your address book, and your calendar. All
of these capabilities were very cool and still exist in the
current version of the iPhone.

It's been almost 30 years since the birth of the Newton. Apple didn't sit idly by during this period. The company introduced another device to store and play your
digital music called the iPod. Apple, being a smart and
innovative company, then combined the Newton with
the iPod and combined that yet again with the ability to
make a phone call (which Apple didn't invent either).
Voilà! You now have a device called an iPhone. Because
Apple is a truly smart company, it succeeded by layer-
ing existing capability into its product in an innovative
manner. This is a classic example of innovation, not invention.

Small Business Marketing Should Be All Digital—WRONG!

The 1990s was the heyday of the dot-com generation. During that time, the business climate was frothy around e-commerce businesses. While consultants like at Ernst & Young weren't the only folks fueling this frothy existence, we did contribute to the craziness. I remember attending these mega-meetings where the e-commerce "gurus" made blanket statements such as "this is a new economy" and "forget everything you know about business because all the rules have changed." I have to believe most of my fellow consultants deeply believed that this was crap, but no one would admit this in fear that we may have been the ones who "didn't get it."

As this played out, everyone started to realize that the "forget everything you know about business" craziness proved to be ridiculous. The e-commerce generation, however, did introduce new ways to engage customers and sell products. But when the dust settled, business was conducted as it had been for a long time.

When I reflect back on my career as the "digital guy," I feel good about my skills and accomplishments. I like to think I added strong value to the companies I worked for. Today those skills are important to me as a small business owner, but I needed that gentle nudge, or maybe not so gentle, to help me have a more balanced perspective on success as a small business owner.

I'm a big fan of digital business, and I feel very passionate about its value. However, with very rare exceptions, no business, especially small business, can survive wholly as a digital business. Even digital businesses such as Amazon.com are realizing that more traditional means to reach their consumers are still viable options.

First, consumers have needs, and businesses need to satisfy those needs. Moreover, businesses need to engage their target markets in the manner that their target consumers want to be engaged. Businesses still need to listen to and understand the needs of their target market. This has been, and still is, Marketing 101.

What has changed is how to interact with your changing target market. Most businesses target a wide demographic range of consumers. As discussed in the previous chapter, this wide range will utilize technology differently. Think of your marketing portfolio like balancing your investment portfolio. Include some marketing strategies using technology that speaks to the younger generations. But also mix in some more traditional means like direct mail that the older generations are more likely to respond to.

Let me use a specific example to illustrate this point. One of the common lead generation techniques used by all Sport Clips owners is to give away free haircuts for first-time customers. If a customer tries our service for free, he will be highly likely to become a repeat visitor because of the exceptional experience.

In this simple example, as a Sport Clips owner, I have two primary ways to distribute free haircut coupons: traditional printed coupons sent through the mail or digital coupons distributed through Facebook. After testing both distribution methods, I can state very strongly that both work but for different reasons. Distributing traditional coupons is hard to scale. Essentially, a person has to physically distribute the coupon, so you're limited by how much you can invest to have someone hand out coupons. Also, distributing the physical coupon isn't very targeted. What I've learned, however, is that even with the weaknesses of a printed coupon, I can expect a 2 percent redemption rate on average. Facebook coupons, on the other hand, can be highly targeted. The downside to Facebook is that the expected redemption rate is unpredictable.

The characteristics of both types of coupons are different. Some of my potential customers respond to traditional coupons, and a different customer base responds positively to digital coupons. If you want to service both, you have to engage with them in the ways they wish to be engaged.

The good news is that you as a small business owner now have a new set of "arrows" in your marketing quiver to reach audiences that previously may have been unreachable.

Big Companies Are Investing to Stay Relevant for the Younger Consumers

This book is designed to address the needs of the small business owner. But the good news is that large companies are heavily investing in digital, which benefits all of us small business owners.

Mega companies such as Ruffles and the Walt Disney Company recognized that their consumer base was evolving. In order to remain relevant to those changing needs, these companies explicitly acknowledged that their consumers prefer "pixels over paper" and have been adjusting their investments accordingly.

Ruffles, a brand of Frito-Lay, is a dramatic example of a brand that has performed a full pivot with their advertising investment (source: www.digiday.com/brands/ruffles-digital). In 2013, two-thirds of Ruffles' advertising budget was spent on television, with only 20 percent spent on digital. In 2014, Ruffles spent 100 percent of its budget on digital, primarily social media ads. The reason for such a dramatic shift? They recognized that their target market (primarily millennials) was consuming more entertainment on their smartphones and not traditional broadcast television. Below is an example Facebook post to give you a flavor for their social media strategy.

While this is a simple post, it illustrates creativity served with a solid touch of entertainment. Also notice the logo in the bottom right-hand corner of the post. Ruffles isn't directly trying to sell you a bag of Ruffles with this post. The company is instead leading with entertainment, not commerce. The number of Likes and Shares indicates that this post was well received. Shares and Likes are one thing, but does this type of marketing shift impact the bottom line? Revenue for Ruffles in 2014 increased 8.19 percent in comparison to 2013. Engage your consumer in the manner your consumer wants to be engaged.

I occasionally get asked if I ever worked on anything famous at the Walt Disney Company. My answer? Yes! It came in the form of *Camp Rock*, a tweener movie released a few years ago. *Camp Rock* pioneered the deliv-

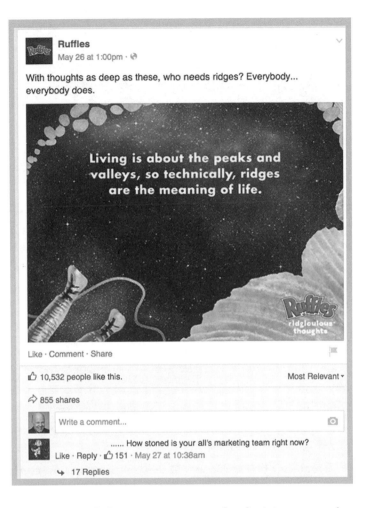

ery of high-definition movies and television over the
Internet.

The Disney Channel wanted to produce *Camp Rock*
so it could be viewed on both traditional broadcast television and over the Internet. This was an explicit ac-
knowledgment by Disney that consumers were starting
to consume entertainment on digital channels.

The wise Disney Channel folks wanted *Camp Rock* to stream, on demand, for 24 hours. This digital launch had to happen at the same time as the movie premier on the Disney Channel. Also, before consulting the digital production teams, Disney Channel ran TV ads announcing this simulcast. The groups responsible for digital production within Disney experienced a corporate freak-out because this type of project had never been successful in the industry. But Disney is rightfully famous for not disappointing its fans.

Freak-out or not, at precisely 9 p.m. (EST), in conjunction with the premier of *Camp Rock* on the Disney Channel, any kid, anywhere in the country, could go to www.disney.com and watch this new movie any time they wanted. My personal satisfaction resulted when I came home after the launch and my then 8- and 10-year-old kids were watching the movie on laptops. This helped define their idea of "normal" television and movie-viewing behavior. Welcome to the wonderful world of working at Disney!

Companies such as the Walt Disney Company have two strengths when it comes to digital. One of those strengths is having very deep pockets. The second strength is having a clear vision of the needs of their target market coupled with a vision of how to satisfy those emerging needs. What does this mean to a small business owner? First, accept the fact that the needs of your consumers are changing and that you need to change with them. The second is don't fret because you don't have deep pockets. Those big-company investments have made it a lot less expensive for small companies to work in this digital space.

Chapter 3
MARKETING IN THIS EVER-CHANGING WORLD

Everyone needs a humbling experience occasionally. No one wants his ego crushed, but those professional slaps in the face usually serve as great learning opportunities. Once you recover from the initial blow to the ego, those situations are actually very healthy.

My humbling, ego-crushing experience was dealt by a $375-a-month, single-color coupon book. About the most low-tech marketing tactic you can imagine.

On the first day of opening my first Sport Clips, a lady came into the store asking for the owner. She introduced herself as the owner of a local coupon book franchise and felt strongly that her coupon book would be of great benefit for acquiring new haircut customers.

I looked at her coupon book, and I must admit I was skeptical. Many coupon books are very high quality, approaching the quality of a magazine. Her book, unfortunately, was not one of those. It was gray scale with a single color. It was also printed on newspaper stock, which is one of the lowest quality papers available. She must have sensed my reaction, so she pointed out to me that consumers only care about the value of the coupons, not four colors on glossy paper. In passing, she mentioned that 100,000 local consumers pick up the book, which then started to spark my interest.

Working for Disney for several years, whether right or wrong, you start to develop a very high expectation of the consumer experience. Many times, that expectation borders on perfection. For the brand called the Walt Disney Company, that's exactly how the brand needs to be perceived. The rest of the real world, however, doesn't need to be obsessed with a near-perfect experience.

There I was with all my Disney background and misguided expectations of perfection; I was staring at this single-color, newsprint coupon book. My reaction was that this would never work. But for whatever reason, I agreed to run a three-month test.

The results started to pour in. At the end of the first month, this coupon book became my highest performing marketing vehicle based on the number of new customers it attracted. Good performance continued through the second month. Toward the end of month three, I signed a 12-month contract.

What lessons did I learn? First, don't have a digital-only, or traditional-only, bias. And second, we as small business owners shouldn't choose how our customers want to interact with us. Listen and learn the needs of your customers and meet them on their terms.

So with this swirl of change and the pace of change, how does a busy small business owner make sense of this new world order, which still has elements of the old world order?

A Framework for Thinking about Your Marketing

A framework is defined as a basic conceptual structure (of ideas). Huh?

I know, this academic definition is a touch abstract, but I'm a real fan of frameworks, so allow me to defend this definition.

A good framework is a way to make order out of chaos. In the small business world of marketing, there are thousands of marketing choices. Complicating these choices are the different types of marketing. For example, you can do brand marketing to raise awareness or transactional marketing to convert potential customers to actual customers. But this enormity of options can be overwhelming. A framework helps organize this complexity in a manner that can help you make decisions.

A good marketing framework is based on a consumer's intent. Are they ready to make a purchase decision, or will they be making that decision in the future? As an example, you've just met someone for the first time, and they ask about your business. You tell them that you own Sport Clips Haircut franchises. If they've never heard of Sport Clips, you explain the business concept. If they mention that they've been looking for a new place to get a haircut, you can give them a free haircut coupon to try out the business. The point is to respond to the need based on where the potential customer is in their understanding and decision-making.

While not limited to just digital marketing, I really like the following framework to inform marketing decisions:

Reach -› Engagement -› Conversion -› Retention

REACH equates to brand awareness. If I am opening a new Sport Clips in a new market, for example, very few of my potential customers will be aware of this thing called "Sport Clips." Questions abound, such as, "Is this a sports team?" or, "Is this a film producer specializing in sporting events?" So the primary communications message needs to explain Sport Clips as a "sports-themed environment focused on a championship haircut experience for men and boys." Obviously, over time, the need for REACH-oriented messaging starts to diminish, but it will never fully go away. With our ever-increasing need for instant gratification and the sensory bombardment coming from media outlets, brand messaging can have a very short shelf life.

ENGAGEMENT attempts to answer the question, "Can I trust you?" Building trust takes time. While the nuances of building trust are very complicated, I fundamentally believe that trust comes from valuing a relationship over a financial transaction. Relationships don't come from constantly communicating "buy now" messaging. No one wants to be constantly sold something.

CONVERSION is a call to action. Asking for certain things such as a sale or a newsletter sign-up. This is the make-or-break point where you're asking a potential customer to become an actual customer. If you've been successful in the prior two phases, your odds during conversion will increase.

RETENTION is when you have a customer and you want to keep that customer. Imagine you own a Sport Clips and you've cut someone's hair for the first time. Sport Clips strives to have every customer feel like they receive the best haircut ever. A great haircut and an amazing in-store experience are critical for return business. But in the spirit of valuing the relationship more than the transaction, you also need to communicate your love for the clients. Things like client-appreciation events and a simple "thank you" go a long way.

Let's Get Busy

Now that you have a way to think about your digital persona, the next chapter is intended to be an inventory of your options. But be warned: I'm going to use a shock-and-awe strategy first, but then I'll safely bring you back to the practical digital world of a real business owner.

Chapter 4
A DIGITAL STRATEGY FOR YOUR LONG-TERM SURVIVAL

One of the digital challenges facing any owner is where to get started. Most have some personal experience with social media like Facebook, but is social media appropriate for business? If you have a social media presence for your business, do you really need a website? The list of questions is almost endless and can be overwhelming.

Organizations that provide digital services to the small business community compound this problem. There are many service providers that prey on the small business owner's lack of understanding. These self-proclaimed "experts" typically do not truly represent the best interest of their customers.

Here's a real example:

A business owner who attended one of my seminars asked me to review a proposal he'd received. This business owner had asked for this proposal because he felt, his website needed a makeover. The look and feel were dated, and he felt with a more modern interface he could increase his online revenue.

The proposal he received from one service provider was a sham. The service provider stated in the proposal that in order to redesign the user interface, they had to host the website, and they needed to replace the mechanisms to take payment. Neither of these changes had anything to do with the user interface. According to the proposal, the reasons for these recommendations were "too technical" to explain. Nowhere did they propose the redesigned website as the business owner requested.

This provider was either incompetent or trying to prey on a business owner who didn't have a complete digital strategy for his business.

I have numerous other examples. It's very common for digital providers of services to small businesses to recommend what they know, or claim to know. If you need a website and someone knows WordPress, that provider will recommend a WordPress website. If you need digital advertising support and your provider knows Google pay-per-click advertising (to be explained shortly), the provider will recommend you need Google pay-per-click advertising. See the pattern?

I'm not against using third parties to help build and support your digital strategy. What I am strongly opposed to, however, is turning your digital strategy over to someone who doesn't have a genuine commitment to the business owner's success. I am not a technical expert on all things digital. My expertise stems from being a small business owner with deep technical roots. This background has afforded me the ability to understand the strategy behind those digital solutions that meet the genuine needs of a business.

The Digital Landscape Is Exploding

New technologies are introduced daily, and existing technologies are quickly evolving. Small business owners don't have the time, or maybe the expertise, to stay abreast of this quagmire of change. If you tried to stay on top of this, here's what I suggest would happen to you:

The number of new technologies is doubling every year. This doubling effect has been occurring for decades and will not slow down. Not wanting your brain matter spread everywhere, I'll simplify your understanding in the next chapter by focusing on those technologies I feel are important for you to run your business.

Chapter 5
DIGITAL TOOLS TO ACQUIRE CUSTOMERS

In this chapter, I'm going to give you digital focus. Having thousands of digital options can be overwhelming. I've created this strategy framework to help you see through the minutiae to what's really important for your business success. This isn't perfect, but based on my firsthand experience at large corporations and now as a small business owner, it does work.

The first three steps of your digital marketing framework can be summarized as, "How do you use digital technology to acquire new customers?"

If Your Business Doesn't Have a Website, Your Business Doesn't Exist

Your website is the mainstay of your digital strategy. If you don't have a website or if it's dated, focus solely on having a site built and focus on nothing else until the site is complete.

I can't take credit for my Sport Clips website (my franchisor provides this to all franchise owners), but let me use this to illustrate some of the strengths:

First, you need a clean and simple design with a convincing homepage. A healthy mix of well-spaced imagery and text makes a site understandable. Also, as you can see, my homepage has content describing our

services. If a potential customer is interested, there's a phone number to call, and we have a map to help someone locate the store. Today's consumers have a short attention span and will usually scan a business's homepage before moving on. Decide what a potential customer would like to know about your business, and then include that information on your homepage.

Along with a simple and clean website design, your website needs to be mobile friendly. It needs to operate properly when someone views your website (e.g., www. yoursite.com) from either a smartphone or tablet. Over 90 percent of my Sport Clips website visitors use either a smartphone or tablet. So if your website doesn't work well on mobile devices, you need to hire a reputable service provider to rebuild it. If you don't, you put 90 percent of your potential new customers at risk.

Do you need an application built specifically for phones and tablets? The simple answer is *probably not*. Most mobile-friendly websites can deliver the same capabilities as those available on mobile applications. The one clear reality is, if you invest in both a modern, mobile-friendly website along with a mobile application, you'll at least double your investment. So first invest in the mobile-friendly website. After that launches, let your customers tell you if you need to make the investment in a mobile application.

Remember, invest in a mobile-friendly website or redesign. Do not proceed without it.

If Potential Customers Can't Find You with Search, You Don't Exist

Search engines such as Google and Bing have become the primary means for consumers to locate businesses and research products or services. Consumers who use search engines typically focus only on the first page of the results. So your goal with search engines is to have your business appear on the first page of results, if not the actual first result. Once your business is landing on the first page of search results, your cost to acquire new customers from that channel is essentially free.

Here's a real example where Google search was a hindrance—not a help—to my business growth. I call this issue the "Centre Point Commons" nightmare.

After opening my first Sport Clips in Bradenton, Florida, and with me being digitally sensitive, I was diligently watching search results, hoping to rocket to the number-one spot on the first page of search results. Weeks and months passed with dismal results and no change. If you searched on "haircut men Bradenton," my store was nowhere to be found.

Here's what we learned about this issue. Google favors local businesses in search results. If someone's looking for a haircut in Bradenton, they're going to search with something like "haircut Bradenton." This makes perfect sense.

Google knows where your business is located by what you tell them. You give Google your address as an example. Along with the address, you describe your business on your website. It's also very common to give location information. For example, center name and anchor stores. Centre Point Commons was the name of the retail center where the store was located. Unfortunately, we used "Centre Point Commons" many times on the website homepage. We used it so often Google thought that "Centre Point Commons" was an important location description. Probably no consumer in Bradenton (with the exception of our landlord) knew the name of that center. To test this theory, I searched "haircut Centre Point Commons," and lo and behold, my website rocketed to the number-one position.

The solution was simple. Completely eliminate all references to "Centre Point Commons," which left "Bradenton" as the important location description term. As of the writing of this book, my store in Bradenton has rocketed to the top of both Google and Bing search results.

Here's a screen shot after the change was made:

This isn't position number one, but this store is now on the first page of the results.

Understanding and working with search engines is complicated and ever-changing. Search engines are getting more and more sophisticated.

Complete books have been written on the nuts and bolts of working with search engines, which I do not intend to replicate here. However, I do want to (1) arm you with the basics, and (2) provide enough of my "developed in the trenches" understanding so that you will feel comfortable wading into the search engine stew.

As a business owner, there are two ways to engage with search engines. One is considered organic and is free (search engine optimization). The other is a pay-to-play model (search engine marketing). Search engine optimization is where you design and build your website to work best with search engines. Search engine marketing, on the other hand, is where you pay the search engines for search terms to enhance your results.

So what to do if you're a small business owner? I like free, so I strongly suggest you don't worry about search engine marketing and keep your money in your pocket. Instead, give the search engines what they expect and need. Make it easy for them to understand your business.

Working with search engines is complicated, but there are only two you need to worry about. The biggest and most influential is Google, with Microsoft's Bing being a distant second. The good news is that, in general, if you can make Google happy, Bing will be happy as well.

Short of paying search engine experts a lot of money, what's a small business owner to do? Go to the Google search engine and search on this exact phrase "search engine optimization best practices 201x" (x is for the current year) and look at the results. While you'll see a gazillion results, the one that is most interesting will be a document published by Google. While Google won't give you all the secret sauce, it will tell you how to help them be successful understanding your business. Read that document and methodically implement (where you can) Google's recommendations. You might not fully understand some of the recommendations. If so, then and only then hire a search engine specialist to help you implement just that recommendation. If you do hire someone, don't allow yourself to be upsold.

This may sound like an overly strong business requirement, but with search engines becoming such a strong and growing force, you shouldn't ignore this customer acquisition strategy. If you're willing to roll up your sleeves and do this type of work, I'm confident that the search engine gods will reward you.

All You Need Is One Good Social Media Platform (to Start)

A few years ago, I was speaking with an MBA student, asking his thoughts on the exploding number of social media options. His response was profound. You only need one good social network that works for you. To this day, I still think this applies to small business owners as well.

Social media initially was focused on individuals, and many people have their personal pages to keep in touch with friends and family. Now these same social media platforms have capabilities for businesses. Instead of friends and families, these business pages focus on customers and potential customers. This discussion is focused solely on business capabilities.

If you believe that simplicity is the best strategy, then the decision over which social platform to choose can be simple. If your customers and potential customers are consumers, use Facebook. If your customers are other businesses, use LinkedIn. Why? These two platforms have the highest number of users. You can, rightfully so, make the argument that not all of your customers use those platforms—no marketing channel will ever reach 100 percent of your target market. Don't worry about it. Financially, it usually makes sense to invest in the channel that can give you the broadest reach—either Facebook or LinkedIn.

The other reason I suggest focusing on just one solution is a point of practicality. Being active on social media requires a lot of work. Most small business owners don't have enough time to manage multiple solutions. True, you can hire someone to manage your social presence, but there are limitations to this strategy that will be discussed later.

I like simplicity when it comes to social media, but as usual, there is an exception to "focus on one" recommendation. If your business is highly visual (e.g., architect, artist, or designer) you'll need to be drawn to the more visual platforms such as Instagram or Pinterest. If you own one of those types of businesses, consider first building a Facebook (or LinkedIn) presence. Once you're comfortable with your first platform, then add on either an Instagram or a Pinterest.

Facebook and LinkedIn are very similar, just focused on different target markets. So not to overwhelm you with redundancy, for the remainder of the book I'm going to discuss Facebook. Rest assured, what I describe for Facebook will have a strong corollary in LinkedIn.

Social Platforms Are About Being Social, Not Selling

Facebook is by far the largest social media platform, period. You may or may not have a personal page, but a massive number of folks on this planet do. A lot of your customers and potential customers are using Facebook. Engage your customer base the way they want to be engaged. This is clearly a compelling argument for a consumer-oriented small business to have a business Facebook presence. The very good news is that Facebook has realized that the small business segment is very profitable, so they are investing heavily in tools for small business owners. As an example, Facebook has an amazingly powerful paid advertising capability that can enable any small business to reach their target market with surprising precision.

But social platforms are just that: social. The first objective for using social platforms for business purposes is to engage with your followers. As a business using Facebook, you first need to "be a real person." People will not be social with a business, but they will be social with another human. Likewise, no one wants to be sold something constantly, either in Facebook or in real life.

So how do you develop a "human" voice on social media? The answer to that question is very personal based on what you're comfortable with. So let me give you some examples:

This cool kid haircut picture was taken by one of the stylists in our store. It's not professionally produced, but it does illustrate the social aspect of Facebook. Moms love their kid's picture on Facebook. Every mom thinks their kid is the coolest, so why wouldn't they want to share their perfect child with friends and family? Notice the "people-reached" metric. When I post a cool kid's haircut, you can see the precise moment when the Mom sees the post. The people-reached metric starts to skyrocket. Good post!

The second example is an example of a not-so-good post, as you can see by the people-reached metric. This is a professionally produced post that on the surface seems to be relevant to a predominately male target market. I've posted other similar types of posts and invariably they perform poorly. Is this poor performance a result of the post being professionally produced or because guys don't like to read articles about haircuts? It's unclear, but I suspect both factors influence this type of poor performance. I don't recommend completely shying away from professional content. Just don't rely on this type of content for all your social posts. Look for those "cool kid haircut" types of opportunities in your business.

Sport Clips Bradenton - Centre Point Commons
Published by iAPPS Social (SportClips) [?] · April 28 · 🌐

7 Men's Hairstyles for Short Hair
Here are some ideas is you're considering a shorter cut for our hot summer months.
http://bit.ly/1O9VOqs

7 Men's Hairstyles for Short Hair

Short haircuts are easy to wear and have style. Check out these pictures of men's hairstyles for short hair for 7 cool and on trend looks.

MENSHAIRSTYLETRENDS.COM

This next example is a simple photograph of a pylon sign taken before we opened one of our stores. It's a very simple post, but with 112 people reached, I consider this effective. This content was free with the exception of about a minute of my time to take the photo and create the post. Pretty good return on investment!

This next example was a surprise. While this is highly produced, it was a contest giveaway and an entertaining video. Both giveaways and video are known to perform well, but this was just an okay post. My suspicion about the performance was that the post image could have been more appealing. Regardless, that's how you learn what works on Facebook.

Before I close this discussion and transition to online advertising, I'll leave you with this. Regardless of what specific content resonates with your audience, always show your audience that there's a real human behind the post and not a business entity. Humans like to socialize with humans, not businesses.

The Basics of Online Advertising Are the Same As Traditional Advertising

Here are the types of questions you ask with any type of advertising: What is your objective? Who do you want to reach? What advertising medium will give you the most value for your investment? Can your advertising creatively grab the attention of your audience?

Websites and social media platforms sell advertising inventory (i.e., a place to run your ad). Just like a magazine can sell you the inside cover of its magazine, a website can sell you space on its homepage for a similar ad. This example is a screen shot of www.msn.com. In this example, you can see an ad paid for by Payless Shoes. MSN decided to make some of the www.msn.com homepage available for paid advertisements. Payless Shoes agreed to pay them to advertise their shoes.

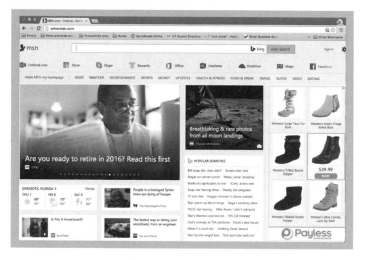

While very similar to traditional advertising, online advertising does present some advantages as compared to traditional mediums. Websites and social media platforms like Facebook know a lot about your behavior and background. Think for a minute about what Facebook knows about you. They keep and analyze every post you make, every friend you connect with, and every Facebook page you view. Television or radio stations, however, don't even know when you are watching one of their shows or listening to one of their broadcasts.

Online advertising provides you with the ability to target with truly phenomenal precision. For example, you're selling dog food and want to advertise on Facebook. You know that only dog owners buy your products (duh!) and that women are more likely to make the purchase decision. So when you post your dog food ad on Facebook, you have Facebook deliver that ad to dog owners who are female. These types of targeting options are almost endless and growing daily.

At this point, I always get questions and freak-outs about online privacy violation. If sites like Facebook know so much about me, are my personal and private data secure? Privacy breaches can occur in any industry. No one can make guarantees, but having been on the corporate side of privacy, I do have a perspective. The major players in this online advertising space are top brands, such as Disney, Facebook, and Google. If for any reason they were responsible for a legitimate privacy breach, they literally could go out of business. Also data privacy in these types of companies is highly regulated and monitored. I consider my private data safe in their hands. While these online companies know a lot about all of us, they never specifically provide insight like your name and address. They aggregate the data such that none of us can be personally identified.

So start slowly with online advertising. You'll develop your own firsthand knowledge of the data, how it's being collected, and how it's being used.

Let me use some examples to illustrate different types of Facebook advertising as compared to more traditional means.

This first example is a brand awareness example. As a small business owner, I could advertise my business by buying billboard space in the outfield of a minor league baseball stadium. You'll know the cost of the billboard as well as some broad statistics around how many folks come to the stadium over the course of a season. You won't know, however, what percentage of those baseball fans will be your target market. It's very hard to measure the true value.

Alternatively, you could invest in a Facebook ad with a razor-sharp targeting. This next ad was intended to make moms aware that our store exists. The logic? moms have kids and kids will need haircuts. This ad ran for a single day on Mother's Day. Besides razor-sharp targeting, there are two things I like about this ad. The first is that the ad didn't ask the moms to bring their sons in for haircuts (no selling). The second is that the image is highly relevant for Mother's Day. The cost of this ad was $25 and I considered this a major hit!

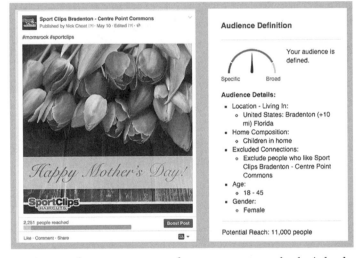

As another compare-and-contrast example, let's look at newspaper ads versus Facebook ads.

Newspaper ads have been around probably since the beginning of newspapers. People do still read newspapers, but readership is on the decline. Regardless, the total readership numbers can still be large (i.e., with a good reach). So, one option for a small business owner is to place an ad in a newspaper.

People will see your ad in a newspaper. The demographic for newspapers is older, so you won't be reaching younger generations like the millennials, however. Unlike Facebook, where users can share content with their friends, newspaper content cannot be shared. Finally, while you'll have newspaper subscription data to inform your decision, that data will give you no insight into your target market. Not bad, but the value will be hard to measure.

On Facebook, however, I can be very specific about who sees an ad.

This is a brand ad focused on high school guys needing prom haircuts. As you can see in the illustration, this ad had very specific targeting. Also, I was able to find this cool photograph taken around the time that this target market's dads would have been in high school. Targeting coupled with a relevant image resulted in a lot of engagement with the ad. I spent $50 on the Facebook ad, and I would estimate the cost of an equivalent newspaper ad to be in the hundreds of dollars.

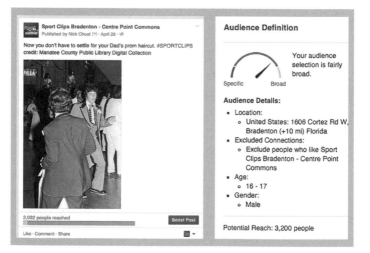

While I'm trying to make a case for the value of razor-sharp targeting, sometimes that's not always the most valuable approach.

I have a growing fondness for Valpak mailers in certain markets. Valpak delivers coupons designed to convert a prospect into a customer. This illustrates that Facebook (and social ads in general) may not always be your best choice for customer conversion.

Assume that you as a business owner want to get a discount coupon to your customers. You can use Valpak to deliver the coupon, or Facebook. Valpak will not give you limited targeting, but Facebook will provide you razor-sharp targeting.

You would naturally assume that razor-sharp targeting would be more effective, but that's not necessarily true. Razor-sharp targeting in Facebook can and does deliver higher engagement with your ad. That doesn't mean that those highly engaged Facebook users will come into your store with your coupon. In fact, my data is very mixed. In some markets, Facebook outperforms Valpak (or other coupon options) and in some markets, it doesn't.

The good news is that the solution is a simple math calculation. How much did you spend to reach a roughly similar-sized target market divided by the number of coupons converted? This is a classic cost of acquisition metric. Run a comparison test to see what works for you and go with the winner.

You can waste a lot of time and money with online advertising if you don't know what works for your business. Let me tie this to the marketing framework of (1) reach, (2) engagement, (3) conversion, and (4) retention. Here's the big reveal: With well-thought-out and relevant creative imagery or video, online advertising crushes traditional advertising for reach and engagement. You will probably, however, have cheaper options for conversion, such as traditional coupons like Valpak. You can amp up your online advertising for conversion, but the ad has to be highly relevant. Finally, the online environment is a wonderful tool for customer retention, but I'm not convinced you need to pay to reach your current customers. Today, you don't have to pay to talk to your customers; why should you in the online world?

If You Ignore Online Directories, You Will Leave Money on the Table

Online directories are a broad description for essentially everything else digital. Although, technically, not all of these platforms are directories. While I don't have hard data, intuitively I believe that 10-20 percent of your digitally acquired new customers will come through these platforms.

You should never assume how people will find your business. As an example, just because you might not use Yelp doesn't mean some of your potential new customers don't. If you ignore these platforms, you risk constricting the number of new customers by 10-20 percent.

One platform, Google for Business (formerly G+), stands out from this crowd for the simple reason that Google owns the platform. The original G+ struggled to capture social hearts and minds like Facebook. So Google, being a smart company, repositioned G+ to be a tool for small businesses instead of a social tool for the masses. Now they call it Google for Business. What is becoming more and more apparent is that Google is using Google for Business to drive small business search results. Bluntly put, if you don't have a Google small business page, Google will punish you by not showing your business in search results. Likewise, if your business has a strong Google for Business presence (i.e., a lot of customer reviews), Google will reward you in search results. If you only implement one of these platforms, make sure it's Google for Business.

Along with Google for Business, there are dozens and dozens of these sites. Many of them you've probably never heard of. How do you get started? The first step is to create your list of target directories. We talked about Google for Business being mandatory. I also would include Bing and Yahoo on that mandatory list because of their popularity. To build the rest of your list, search on "top online directories" or something similar. You should target about 12 or 15 total. As a rule of thumb, if you recognize the name of a directory, add it to your list. In the end, just use your best judgment because there is no perfect answer. When your list is at 15 directories, you can stop.

I have three basic rules for working with these directories. The first—and by far most important—is for you as the business owner to claim your business on those platforms. By claiming your site, you will be telling the directory that you and only you are the business owner. Each directory will have a vetting process to confirm your ownership, but this step is essential. Once you are confirmed as the owner, you will have control of that directory site for your business. You can update content, respond to reviews, and view the analytics to see how many people use that directory. Claiming the first directory will take longer because it will be new, but after you've claimed the first one, it will take you between 15 and 30 minutes to claim the rest. It's actually a pretty solid return on your time spent.

The second rule is to adopt a "set it and forget it" mentality. Actively engaging with your 12 to 15 platforms will cause your workload and head to explode. And with these platforms only generating 10-20 percent of your business, the return on investment would just not be there. So claim the site, load the basic content (e.g., hours of operation, phone number, address...), and don't worry. For the important sites like Google for Business, periodically go to those sites and monitor the reviews and the analytics. For the lesser sites, don't spend any more time after you've completed the initial setup.

The final rule is never to pay for anything. Most of these sites offer a premium subscription service (e.g., $5 per month). If you endorse the mindset of "set it and forget it" as opposed to active engagement, you won't have any need for the premium services. You'll get plenty of value from the free version. Sometimes finding the free capability can be tricky. To quickly find the free version, search with a phrase like this: "free yelp/foursquare...for business."

Claiming and populating these platforms can be some work. So, methodically work down the list until completed, even if it takes a few weeks. Remember, you're trying to unlock that remaining 10-20 percent of your new digitally acquired customer list. The good news is that these directories ask you for the same content. For example, all sites want your address, phone numbers, and hours of operation. They also will want to know your website address and address of your primary social platform like Facebook or LinkedIn. Finally, most of these platforms will let you upload your logo and interior and exterior pictures. Create a central repository of all of this content so that you can just copy and paste into each directory. This will speed up the process and also ensure consistency across all the directories. You can thank me later!

Chapter 6
DIGITAL TOOLS TO RETAIN YOUR CUSTOMERS

The cost to retain your hard-earned customers is much less than the cost to acquire them. A satisfied customer is more likely to refer your business to a friend, family member, or colleague, so having things in place to manage your current customers can yield exponential benefits.

This chapter discusses the two broad strategies for customer retention. The first strategy, "Operational Excellence," has no direct bearing on your digital strategy. The second strategy, "Listen to Your Customers," can be directly impacted by your digital strategy.

Operational Excellence

This may be obvious, but it still bears repeating. The best way to retain your hard-earned customers is to provide an exceptional customer experience. Regardless of your specific business, delighting your customers will reward you with a strong and loyal repeat-customer base. Whether you have a commodity business or a business that has a highly focused niche market, happy customers yield long-term business growth.

Operational excellence is very specific to your business, but let's draw from a few examples to make this point.

I'm a huge fan of Costco Wholesale. I first started shopping there because I could save some serious money. I would suggest their key competitive differentiator isn't price, however. Have you ever directly interacted with a Costco employee in one of their stores? My interactions always have been very positive. They're always helpful and pleasant to deal with, especially if you need to return a purchase. Saving dollars coupled with employees who care are the two Costco differentiators. I truly enjoy the experience and as such have zero motivation to shop at any of Costco's competitors. I'm a Costco consumer for life.

I'm not going to give away all my competitive advantages, but like Costco, one of my key Sport Clips differentiators is the personality of the hair stylists. Do they engage with their customers? Do they make the customers feel comfortable and welcome? Do they make a customer feel like the most important customer to our business? You can train someone to cut hair, but you can't train someone to have a personality.

Here's a larger scale example of operational excellence designed to delight customers. Most of you have visited one of the Walt Disney Parks. I can assume that your experience was outstanding, if not amazing. The Disney Parks are very complex operations, and the design and thought leadership of the Park's guest experience have evolved over decades. Most businesses will never be as complex as Disney Parks, but you can still learn from this world-class operation.

When you visited the Park, did you notice how clean everything was? Maybe you did or maybe you didn't.

Disney has an obsession with cleanliness, and this isn't because Disney employees are clean freaks. The reason for this obsession is simple. People normally don't notice clean surroundings. In fact, everyone expects a business to be clean. You do notice, however, unclean surroundings. Noticing unclean surroundings will distract you from "having fun." Think about the simplicity of this obsession and how it applies to all businesses. The beauty of this is that you don't need an MBA or PhD in computer science. You just need to establish cleanliness standards and the culture and processes to enforce those standards.

Here's another Disney example. Disney has proven that guest satisfaction increases dramatically if guests interact directly Disney Park's employees. This isn't by chance. Disney Park's employees are highly trained to interact with guests and to deal with any situation that could arise. This training is very subtle and hard to notice, very much like actors on a stage. With over 60,000 employees in Disney Parks worldwide, you can't leave this type of guest interaction to personality alone, unlike the Costco and Sport Clips examples. With that many employees, Disney has to "script" the interaction through training. The outcome is the same. Guests, clients, and customers all respond positively when interacting with pleasant and helpful employees.

Is your business delivering with operational excellence designed to delight your customers? If you can't answer that question, you should spend some strategic thinking time to create a list of things that you'd like to change in your business. Prioritize that list and develop an implementation plan to role out those changes incrementally. Once you've implemented a change, measure the success of that change. Did the change meet your expectation? There are many ways to measure operational success. The approach I'm most fond of is listening to your customers.

Listen to Your Customers

How do you know if your business is delighting your customers? You ask them. In the traditional world, your customers are standing in front of you when you talk to them. Don't be overbearing, but just ask them about the experience. They'll tell you.

In the digital world, however, your customers are not standing in front of you. If you follow my advice in this book, however, you can still listen to your customers' feedback. Whether it's leaving a Google for Business or Facebook review, your customers will be speaking to you and to a much larger audience.

This amplified effect of social media is real. If the feedback is praise, a lot of folks will hear the good words. If negative, however, a lot of folks will hear the complaint. You as the business owner can control whether either scenario is positive or negative. If someone praises your business, thank him or her. Likewise, if someone complains, deal with the complaint. Both of these types of responses need to be conducted in the public forum of social media.

Here's a real world example. We have a customer named "Leo." Unfortunately, Leo's first haircut experience was less than satisfactory. After the haircut, Leo wrote a nasty review on Facebook. I was made aware of the review around 9:40 in the morning. I called my wife, as she was responsible for store operations. She called Leo immediately and offered to correct Leo's haircut. Leo agreed to come back to the store that same morning. He arrived at the store around 10:05, five minutes after we opened. Leo received a haircut reservice and by 10:30 that morning retracted his original review and wrote the following review:

> **Leo** — ⭐ **5.0** I have had the best haircuts at this place. not only is every hairstylists amazing at what they do, they're focus is customer satisfaction, Debbie will be my go to stylist for every occasion I have, this is definitely one of the best places I have ever gone to get a haircut and HIGHLY recommend it to everyone. great team with great experience. they really know how to make a Guy feel great about being a guy. sports clips, you guys ROCK!!!
>
> Like · Comment · about a month ago · 2 Reviews · 🌐
>
> 👍 Laura Robinson likes this.
>
> **Sport Clips Bradenton - Centre Point Commons** Thank you for the kind review. We really appreciate your business.
> Like · Reply · Commented on by Michelle Sellars [?] · May 16 at 7:12am

If we hadn't taken immediate action, Leo's original, very negative review would have been seen by dozens of his Facebook friends, plus anyone that came to our Sport Clips Facebook page. I think it's fair to assume that no one who saw his negative review ever would have come into Sport Clips for a haircut. The longer the negative review was posted, the greater the impact. Leo is now one of our strongest supporters.

The negative consequences of not monitoring the digital aspects of your business can be damaging. Unlike a digital directory where you can claim it once and essentially forget it, social networks like Facebook are constantly changing. You need to monitor your Facebook page, and this requires work on your part.

The secret to monitoring your digital business is called "alerts" or "notifications." Once you enable alerts or notifications, the platforms will notify you of any or all types of activities. These alerts or notifications happen immediately, which can really interrupt what you're doing. But interruption or not, you will know about the event and not be surprised. Once you've been made aware, you can then choose when to deal with the situation if that's required.

You have a choice. Either pay attention and engage in the digital conversation, or let the digital conversation start to control your business. Like listening to a customer in your store or restaurant, pay attention to the digital world around you.

Chapter 7
HOW TO GET STARTED

Implementing the digital strategy of your business will not, and should not, happen overnight. It takes time to learn the more mechanical aspects of digital (e.g., how to post on Facebook). Also, it takes time and mistakes to learn what actually works for your business.

Before I recommend a step-by-step implementation, you need to first check your mindset. Are you fully committed to grow this aspect of your business? Do you accept that this will be frustrating and you'll make mistakes? If you're still not mentally prepared, I suggest that instead of disregarding this entirely, try my recommended first step and then judge the results.

I suggest you get started by tackling these activities one at a time, in order.

Develop a Professional Website That Works with Mobile Devices

If you don't have this already, be prepared to spend some money. But this investment, if done properly, will generate good business benefits as well as provide the foundation for future growth.

Most business owners have to hire a third party to build their websites. Select your provider very carefully, and if you don't feel you have the expertise to make an intelligent selection, hire an objective third party to manage this selection on your behalf. If you select the wrong organization to build your website, you can easily waste a lot of money.

One of the requirements for your third-party provider will be to have them build one website that is both traditional as well as mobile friendly. The cost to build a site capable of both will be slightly more expensive than the cost of a traditional site, but much less expensive than the cost to build two sites. The maintenance cost for building a single website that is mobile friendly will also be dramatically less than building separately. The term to use when requesting this is called "responsive design." Also, when you start talking to service providers, make it clear that you only want a mobile-friendly website and not a mobile application that will be downloaded from the application stores.

Make Sure Your Website Is Search Engine Friendly

Free marketing is good marketing. Getting your site to be search engine friendly may not be entirely free, but once your site is search engine friendly, those benefits will be returned to you every day.

If you need to build or rebuild your website, make search engine friendliness a part of your website contract. If you already have a good website that is mobile friendly, heed my suggestion from earlier in the book to lean on Google to guide you through this process. You can either implement the Google suggestions yourself or hire this work out to a third party. If you do hire this work out, have the third party implement all of the Google selections.

After the initial investment, monitor your search performance every few months. If you see your performance degrade, check back with Google to see if they've made any changes. If so, update your site to accommodate those changes.

The return on this investment is tremendous. Once your site is performing well, every time your potential customers search for your product or service, your business will be front and center. This yields benefits 24 hours per day, seven days a week.

Register Your Business with the Top 10-15 Online Directories

This mostly "set it and forget it" strategy is a pain. There are many companies that would love to charge you a small fortune to do this on your behalf. As painful as this process is, resist the urge to pay someone to do the work on your behalf. Think of this as a one-time investment that you need to make.

Setup Google for Business and Bing first. Both are very important for your overall digital success. Also, you can use those two to hone your approach for the others.

You're now left with, as painful as it may be, setting up these directories yourself. As I advised earlier, have a process where you can methodically implement these directories one at a time. Remember, as you set these up, turn on alerts or notifications so that you'll be made immediately aware of activity on those platforms.

I have folks ask me, "Why bother? How many potential customers use these arcane directories?" First, platforms like Google for Business and Yelp aren't that arcane. A lot of people use those platforms. For the others, I see the value proposition as follows. Assume it takes about 30 minutes to register your business with each directory. By the way, if you're organized, 30 minutes is a good estimate. Then assume you get at least one new customer through each directory. Depending on how much you value your 30 minutes, this seems to be a good return on investment. Also, the opportunity to acquire new customers exists as long as the directories remain in business.

Get Social with Your Social Platforms— Content and Entertainment Are Critical

Be human.

This could be the most complicated and costly activity for you to enter into. This is also a hard topic to make definitive recommendations. So let me break this down into two, somewhat related points.

The first point is to develop the social voice of your company. Because social media is about being social, your business will need to develop a voice that resonates with your audience. Based on my experience, the best posts are the ones that aren't overly produced. People react socially to humans and humans typically aren't over produced. The last time I checked, none of us were perfect, so having perfect or near-perfect posts doesn't demonstrate a human persona.

Your fans want to know that there's a human behind the business and not a nameless, faceless corporation. I've found my best "human" metric is whether or not I personally get enjoyment from my social activity. Along with my "human" metric, the social platforms will give you real metrics that will provide feedback on how well you're doing.

Outsource this work or not? I have a bias for this recommendation, but it's an ironic bias. I am a big fan of using third-party consultants. If your business has a specific problem requiring unique expertise, hire a consultant with that expertise. After they solve your problem, they move on to another project. In today's world, however, your social activity should be an ongoing part of your business operations, not a point-in-time project. Also, inserting a consulting firm between yourself and your customers will insulate you from your valuable customers, which isn't a healthy way to run your business. A lot of business owners don't know how to get started, however. Platforms like Facebook are not rocket science. Attend a training class or get some online training. You'll quickly find out how to get started. Once you're engaged, try things and learn from your successes and failures.

Finally, start with one, and only one, primary social platform. Whether that's Facebook or LinkedIn, have that one really good platform and don't get distracted by the endless number of other options. I guarantee your workload will thank me for this recommendation.

Experiment with Pay-to-Play on Social

Once you're comfortable engaging on your social platform, look for opportunities to amp up your social performance. I'm a big fan of using ads in social platforms,
with one exception. Paid social ads work very well in
the first three phases of the marketing framework. If,
for example, your business is a new brand in your market, pay for some brand awareness promotional ads to
get the word out. Also, if you'd like to generate some
leads for your business, pay for a social ad to promote
thought leadership content in exchange for e-mail ad-
dresses.

What these paid ads are awful, or moderately bad,
at is directly driving a sale into your business. Research
has proven this to be true, but I would suggest there's a
human nature aspect to this phenomenon. People don't
want to be "sold" in a social setting. I call this crossing
the social line. People use social networks to be social,
not to be sold things.

What's missing from this recommendation is all of the
other paid advertising options available to you. Those
options are very valid options. But I suggest learning
with Facebook or LinkedIn first and then expanding
your horizons. If you can't make paid ads work for your
business on those two sites, they're probably not going
to work anywhere.

Focus and Enjoy Yourself!

Now that we are approaching the end of this digital journey, I hope I've armed you with some insight that can help you get started on the digital side of your business. Like any new skills, it will take time and focus to make those skills a habit. Early on, pay specific attention and explicitly make digital a part of your operational activities. Over time, these new activities will become second nature. Remember, this isn't rocket science, but you need to apply yourself so that you'll progress through your learning curve.

I agree that some of the activities I've suggested are borderline drudgery. Those boring activities, if you apply yourself, will return real benefits. For the rest of the activities like social media engagement, relax and have fun. I know when I first got active in social media, I was pretty anxious. Was I making the proper posts? Did I have a perfect photo to post? In retrospect, that anxiety was without merit. My relearning that humans are not expected to perfect, even in social media, enabled me to drop the anxiety and just enjoy myself.

Good digital luck!

ABOUT THE AUTHOR

Nick Choat is an entrepreneur, consultant, and speaker with over three decades of professional experience, most recently as a digital strategist. He has held executive positions with highly respected brands such as The Walt Disney Company, Ernst & Young Consulting, the Boeing Company, and VeriSign. He is currently a multi-unit franchisee of Sport Clips Haircuts, leading the expansion of the franchise brand throughout southwest Florida. He regularly speaks on digital strategies for small businesses and volunteers his time to support and help small businesses grow. Nick and his family live in beautiful Sarasota, Florida.

elevate
publishing

**DELIVERING TRANSFORMATIVE MESSAGES
TO THE WORLD**

Visit www.elevatepub.com for our latest offerings.

NO TREES WERE HARMED IN THE MAKING OF THIS BOOK.

OK, so a few did make the ultimate sacrifice.

In order to steward our environment, we are partnered with *Plant With Purpose*, to plant a tree for every tree that paid the price for the printing of this book.

To learn more, visit www.elevatepub.com/about

PLANT WITH PURPOSE | WWW.PLANTWITHPURPOSE.ORG